Please God...

Don't Let Me Lose All My Marbles!

Coloring Book About

How to Keep Your Brain Healthy as You Age

Aunti Says

Published by ProRisk Press

Box 253, Alberta Beach, Alberta Canada T0E 0A0

Patricia@auntisays.com

Patriciaogilvie.com

Copyright © 2015 Aunti Says

Cover Design © 2015 Cover Designed by Patricia Ogilvie

Stock images from GraphicStock

All rights reserved. No part of this publication may be reproduced or transmitted in any form or by any means, including informational storage and retrieval systems, without permission in writing from the copyright holder, except for brief quotations in a review.

ISBN 978-0-9780520-5-8

Revised Modern 2nd Edition Series Printing 2016

Please God ... Don't Let Me Lose My Marbles!

"Well-being is attained little by little, and nevertheless is no little thing."

DEDICATION

This extraordinary coloring book is inspired by and dedicated to my mother Anne whose greatest fear was losing her marbles. And she did, slowly slowly, yet never forgot my name. Love you momma.

ACKNOWLEDGMENTS

To my husband and biggest supporter enabling us to live a healthy lifestyle.

To my teachers and examples throughout life, who have been integral parts of my dietary and physical exercise inspiration. I love and appreciate you all.

And to the close friends who confided they were scared to death of becoming stressed and feeling they are losing their minds. Stress does this. Here's the story.

Praise for *Please God... Don't Let Me Lose All My Marbles!*

"Congratulations to an awesome person who had a vision and went on to be a super star. This is amazing!

– Christine Nichiporik

"What a delightful, creative and fun way to face color-through fears. We can all benefit from Aunti Says."

- Patricia Morgan

Aunti Says

INTRODUCTION

What is dementia? It's the overall term used for a set of symptoms that are caused by disorders affecting the brain.

The common symptoms include memory loss and trouble problem solving, mood swings, and unusual behavior.

It's not a specific disease, however, it becomes worse as you stress yourself out.

Hell, let's not glaze over this. Stress is the number one culprit that brings on disease, ailments, traumas, and worst of all (in my humble opinion) the sense of losing one's marbles!

Not remembering is a direct correlation to the level of stress you experience in your life.

My research has shown the adult coloring book trend is popular for this very powerful reason – it reduces stress, allows the brain to focus, and when feeling better, one makes better decisions. In fact, one can think again.

So here it is, your coloring booklet about how to keep your brain healthy as you age.

Even though the experts claim that memory loss is a normal condition as we age, other sources prove that stress in everyday life brings on brain weariness and thus, memory loss. But listen, it doesn't have to be this way at all.

Contrary to what many believe, researchers are finding that varying forms of marble loss can be reversed.

The concept of coloring has proven to reduce anxiety and when the focus is on a positive aspect for any duration of time (more than 17 seconds), fears and apprehensions reduce.

It is then, that better decisions are made when anxiety abates. It is then, illness subsides and health has a chance to flourish.

This little book addresses the root causes of forgetting and reminds us how to remember better. It provides mandalas and other pictures to color, inspiring stress relief.

As a lifetime student of applying relaxation and mind soothing exercises and a master of wiping stress out, I've read and tested dozens of the best adult coloring books and studied the psychology of focus on the subject of how to bring health to the mind.

"Please God, Don't Let Me Lose My Marbles" can be taken with you anywhere, add a smile, a pack of cultured pens, pencils or crayons and allow it to take you through a proven process to tap into how to reduce the fears of losing your marbles.

There is room in the margins of the pages for writing in all your C.R.A.P. about forgetting things and slowly increasing Zen energy while changing your mental state from fear to relaxed.

Applying the latest trending books is visionary. Applying trending adult coloring books for a specific issue like fear of dementia is poignant and you should be proud that you are willing to live with a healthy mind.

I promise if you bring my little book into your life, offering a vision and simple plan of action to reduce normal stress, especially over the holidays, you will be surprised and pleased at the results.

What a great idea – mental health solutions to worldwide

problem – brain and worry stress reduction the fun way.

You are probably the kind of person who sees opportunities and one of a kind special soul your family and friends marvel at. I bet you take action immediately.

The concept of coloring to reduce stress is a big-ticket item in today's fast paced hectic world. And you're about to experience a powerful little book to keep your stresses at bay and mind healthier.

This book will guide you page by page to train yourself to focus on positive thoughts long enough for them to manifest and produce more positive thoughts.

The rules are simple: 1. Smile 2. Grab a crayon 3. Trace the words of inspiration. 4. Color the mandalas and pictures.

God answers.

Aunti Says

Please God … Don't Let Me Lose My Marbles!

Can my brain be healed? Can Alzheimer's be prevented? Maybe. Maybe not. But HELL, healthier lifestyle choices will keep my brain healthier and stronger as I age.

Today, I will stop worrying about my future. If I don't, I may continue to lose my marbles.

Please God … Don't Let Me Lose My Marbles!

There are good days and bad days. Today is a good day.

Please God … Don't Let Me Lose My Marbles!

I'm ready to challenge myself. I won't play a game of basketball, but I sure can play cribbage with my friend.

And if my friend is busy, I will dial someone else using my less dominant hand. Hah. Tricking my mind is no trick at all. It's about giving my brain a workout because I love my brain.

Please God … Don't Let Me Lose My Marbles!

God knows, there's enough to worry about without worrying about worrying about things.
— Edward Gorey

Please God … Don't Let Me Lose My Marbles!

One of the best ways to keep my brain healthy is to play a musical instrument.

Playing well with practice may not solve all my problems, but it sure will annoy some of my friends if I keep it up every day.

So I better make it worth the effort!

Please God ... Don't Let Me Lose My Marbles!

Worrying is wrecking my brain!

So today I will do a puzzle to keep my brain healthy.

Because even if I don't know all the answers, I am giving my brain a boost.

Maybe I'll just color the boxes.

Please God … Don't Let Me Lose My Marbles!

		4			3	6	8	2
	8			5				
3		1		6	8	5		
	4							
9		6		4	5		3	8
	7		3	8			6	9
	3	8	5					
				3		8	5	4
5	6		8	7			2	

I love a party. Don't you? I think I'll go dancing and meet some new people. Or I could just take one of my good friends and go for a walk or for a cup of tea. (Or a glass of wine...)

Either way, moving with a friend is very important to keep my brain healthy.

Please God ... Don't Let Me Lose My Marbles!

"Hope" is the thing with feathers -

That perches in the soul -

And sings the tune without the words -

And never stops - at all.

—Emily Dickinson

Please God … Don't Let Me Lose My Marbles!

I really need to stay more active which helps reduce stress, boosts my moods, and keeps my relationships with my loved ones strong.

Oh look. It's raining.

What shall I do?

Let it rain!

Because jumping in a puddle is long overdue.

Please God … Don't Let Me Lose My Marbles!

I always said, "It's never too late to have a happy childhood."

Go jump in the lake. Okay.

Go play in the snow. Okay.

Go fly a kite. Okay.

Laugh and sing. Okay.

Please God … Don't Let Me Lose My Marbles!

You know what's wrong with my friends?

They always complain they are overtired, anxious, compulsive, depressed, worrywarts, and then they tell me it's normal.

You know what I say?

Normal is smiling more and coloring!

Please God ... Don't Let Me Lose My Marbles!

I gotta give my brain a rest. I'm thinking about everything and everyone. Stop! My first lesson today is to remind myself that I hurt myself over and over when I try to please everybody.

Today, I will focus on me and me only. And my kitty cat.

Please God … Don't Let Me Lose My Marbles!

My doctor told me a secret.

She said that eating healthier not only improves my general health, but it helps maintain brain function, slows and even stops memory loss.

Please God ... Don't Let Me Lose My Marbles!

"Eat colors!"

- Blue and purple like blackberries and blueberries and purple cabbage

- Green like avocado, celery, peas

- White, tan and brown like bananas, potato, turnip, garlic

- Orange and yellow like peaches, oranges.

Please God ... Don't Let Me Lose My Marbles!

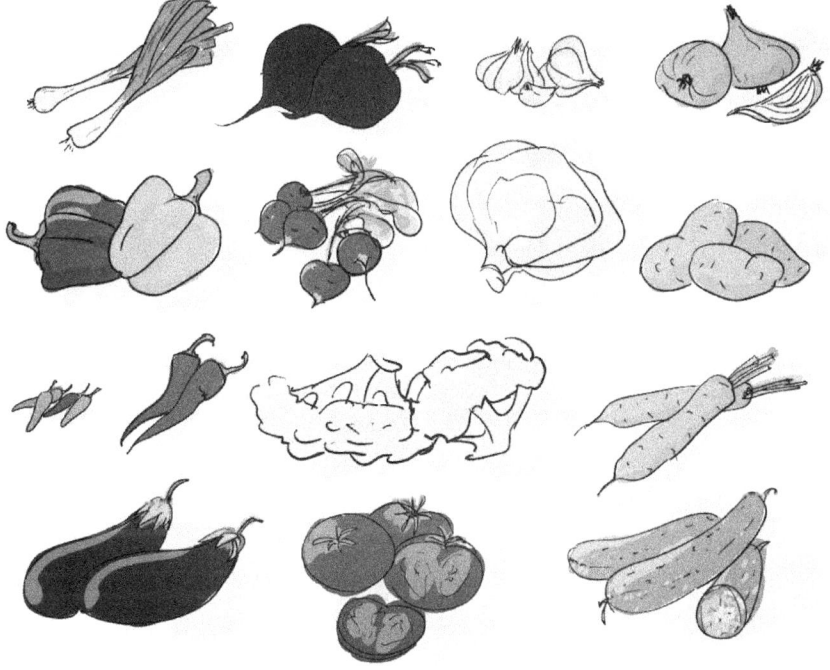

God loves me.

God loves me.

God loves me.

It's not what they take away from me that counts, it's what I do with what I have left.

God Loves Me.

Please God … Don't Let Me Lose My Marbles!

Today I will change my mind about exercise. I will call it "activity" not "exercise" and remind myself that my body needs to move.

I'll walk a little more, climb a little more, and complain a little less. Because I don't want to wreck my brain. I want it healthy and smart.

Please God ... Don't Let Me Lose My Marbles!

I have learned that any happiness I get, I've got to make myself.

My smart doctor keeps telling me that over time, stress causes vascular changes and chemical imbalances that damage my brain and other cells in my body. What causes me the most stress? I shall write them here. Six of them.

Please God ... Don't Let Me Lose My Marbles!

Time to find out more about reducing stress.

There are the regular activities like meditation, deep breathing, massage, nature, oh and find better friends!

Hey, I shouldn't laugh, but if my friends are bullies and talking negative, I need to make a change.

Please God ... Don't Let Me Lose My Marbles!

I'm pretty smart and listen to my body and mind. I will take time today to listen really carefully and make a list of my unrealistic expectations and try to accept what cannot be changed. I will get support.

Be better prepared

- And get more sleep!

Please God ... Don't Let Me Lose My Marbles!

Do I have these stressors?

- Emotional - depression, anxiety, anger, worry?

- Physical - headaches, tired, sweating?

- Mental - can't concentrate, memory loss, confusion?

- Behavioral - fidgeting, alcohol, drugs?

Please God ... Don't Let Me Lose My Marbles!

When I was young I smoked, drank, stayed up late, never got a check-up, and didn't really care if anybody took notice. I ate crap and loved it.

Was that too crazy?

Stop worrying about it and appreciate what I do have that is going well in my life right now. I'm not crazy!

Please God ... Don't Let Me Lose My Marbles!

"Courage is being scared to death and saddling up anyway."
- John Wayne

And I scared to age? Scared to lose my marbles?

Saddle up! So much is being done to cure forms of dementia. But it's my responsibility to take better care of myself.

Please God ... Don't Let Me Lose My Marbles!

I can slow and prevent my brain decline.

But I have to challenge myself everyday.

My brain is a system filled with neurons that respond to my environment and thoughts. By stimulating my mind every day, I can preserve my memory.

If I don't, I kill my brain.

Please God ... Don't Let Me Lose My Marbles!

By now I get it that stress promotes memory loss.

Under too much stress my body produces cortisol. In large amounts this is toxic to my brain cells.

Over time, it shows up as haziness, forgetfulness, and confusion.

Please God ... Don't Let Me Lose My Marbles!

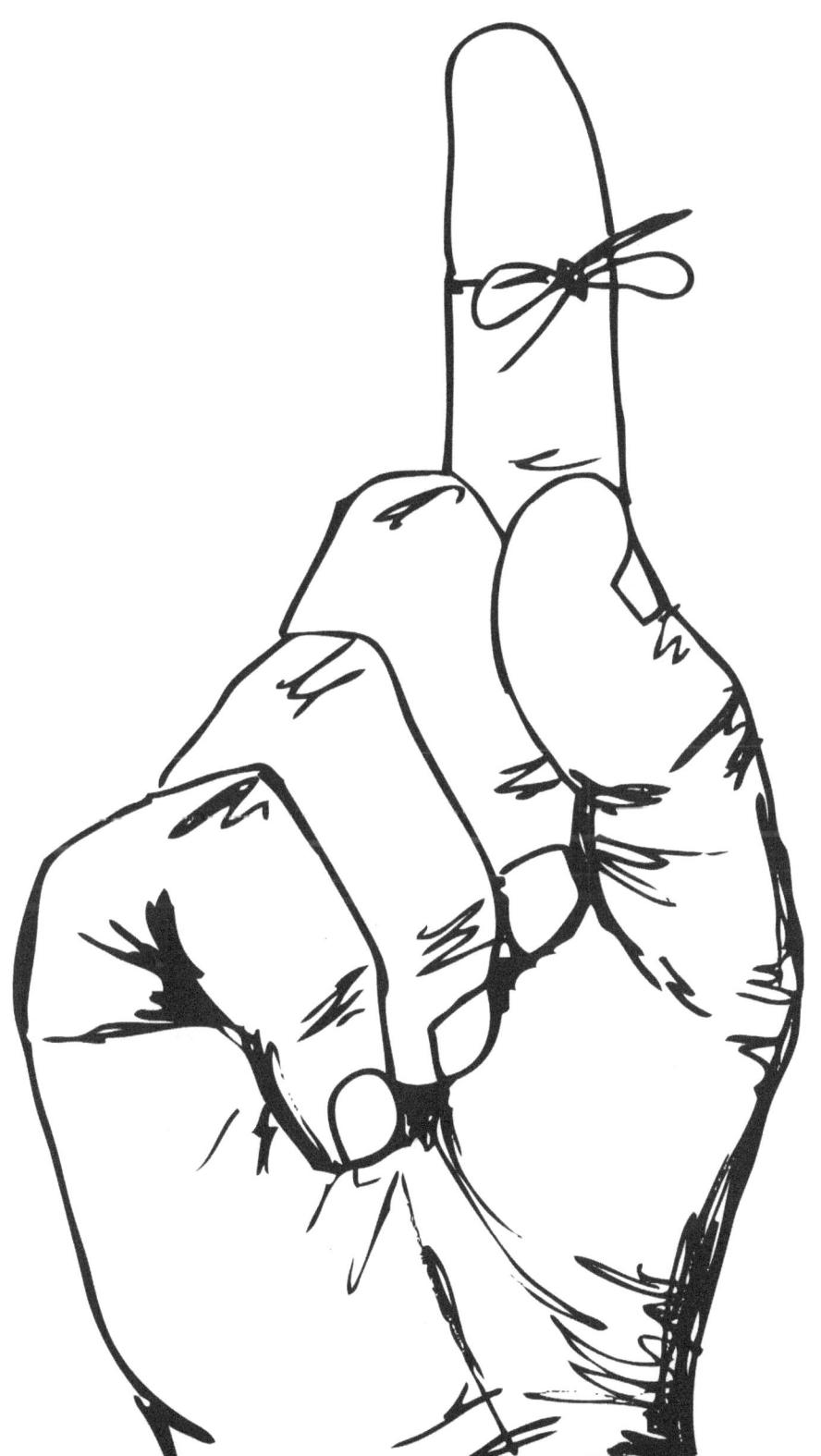

From today on, my daily regime will be to love myself. I will do my best to love myself first, and everything else will fall into place.

I am willing to love and respect myself.

Then I won't stress out so much because I am making decisions that matter best for me.

Please God … Don't Let Me Lose My Marbles!

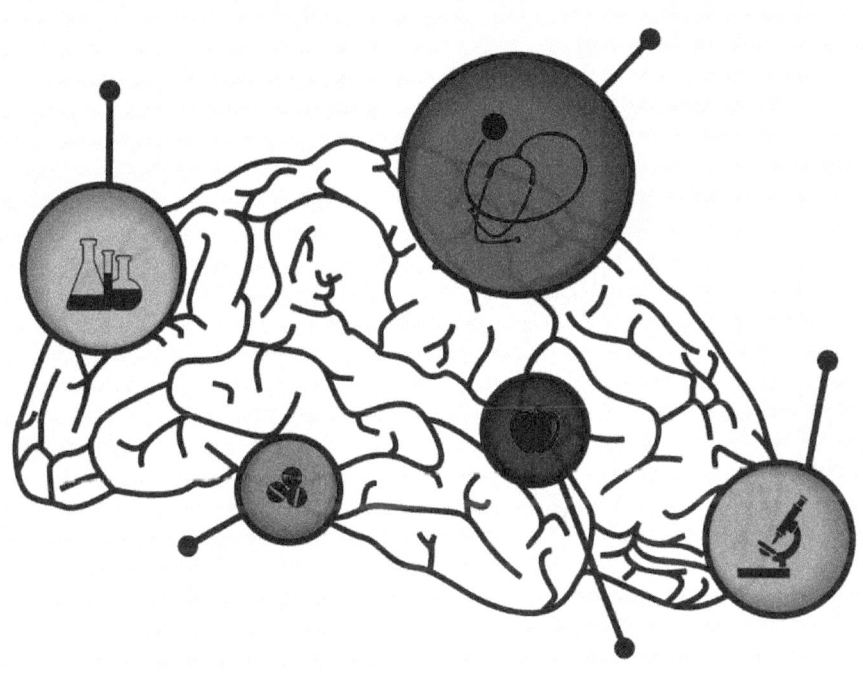

Today I will make a date with myself.

To preserve a youthful mind, I will take a block of time everyday to practice and enjoy relaxation. But today, you and me kid!

It means get the heck out of the house and enjoy my own company.

Please God ... Don't Let Me Lose My Marbles!

Brain Fog. I felt a cloud covering the top of my head and it changed my life. It frightened me and it stopped me from remembering as well as I used to.

I know I can reverse this because I know it came when I was most stressed at home and at work.

Please God ... Don't Let Me Lose My Marbles!

Here are other reasons for brain fog:

- Lack of sleep

- Brain abnormalities

- Premature brain aging

- Mental distraction due to pain or discomfort.

The other word - STRESS!

Please God ... Don't Let Me Lose My Marbles!

Drink water. Interesting that what happens is, when I'm supposed to feel good, I do!

Please God ... Don't Let Me Lose My Marbles!

What else can I do today to keep me hydrated, relaxed, positive, and willing to take better care of myself so I don't lose my marbles?

Have hope because the alternative is what? Despair? Who wants that? Not me! Challenge my brain everyday!

Please God ... Don't Let Me Lose My Marbles!

A panel of experts including a Harvard neurologist agreed that memory loss is NOT a normal part of aging. Hurrah!

The brain responds to the same insults as the body - stress, poor diet, toxins, lack of sleep, lack of physical activity.

Today I do reduce the and put in stuff. I will doctor for and my far

I have noticed after these weeks of coloring and being reminded to take better care of myself, that when I look in the mirror, I see a smiling face.

I am willing to follow these steps to better my brain and reduce (even stop) worrying about losing my marbles.

Please God … Don't Let Me Lose My Marbles!

"If I had my life to live over... I would have more actual troubles and fewer imaginary troubles." - Don Herold

I will be courageous because that is what matters. My courage gets me from one moment to the next.

I can't be that kid standing at the top of the diving board platform, over thinking it.

I have to take the step off and dive head first into the pool of de-stress and self-love.

RESOURCES

Attree EA, Dancey CP, Pope AL. Cyberpsychology and Behavior. 2009 Aug;12(4):379-85. <u>An assessment of prospective memory retrieval in woman with chronic fatigue syndrome using a virtual-reality environment; an initial study.</u>

Dr. Sears about Brain Health:

http://www.alsearsmd.com/category/brain-health

Additional Articles from Dr. Sears about Anti-Aging:

http://www.alsearsmd.com/category/anti-aging/

Spalletta, G., Bernardini, S., Bellincampi, L., et al. (2007). Glutathione S-transferase P1 and T1 gene polymorphisms predict longitudinal course and age at onset of Alzheimer's disease. The American Journal of Geriatric Psychiatry. 15 (10):879-887.

http://drhyman.com/blog/2010/06/14/9-steps-to-reverse-dementia-and-memory-loss-as-you-age-2

"Well-being is attained little by little, and nevertheless is no little thing."

Thank You for Being Here!

If you like this little purse sized adult coloring book, you'll love the 1st and 3rd Adult Coloring Books in this Trilogy of stress reducers and fun increasers.

Look for Bag Lady and Respect in the Series here: Www.auntisays.com/shop/

Please God ... Don't Let Me Lose My Marbles!

www.ingramcontent.com/pod-product-compliance
Lightning Source LLC
Chambersburg PA
CBHW061339040426
42444CB00011B/3000